BLOOD LINES

BLOOD LINES

35 Selected Poems

Lana E. Wolkonsky

VANTAGE PRESS
New York

Published by Vantage Press, Inc.
516 West 34th Street, New York, New York 10001

Manufactured in the United States of America
ISBN: 0-533-11620-1

Library of Congress Catalog Card No.: 95-90581

0 9 8 7 6 5 4 3 2 1

To the eternal goodness of God

. . . and to all those with anger in their hearts
who know not all the beauty
even harsh words and hurtful gestures
can evoke

Contents

About the Author

Lana E. Wolkonsky was born in Lakewood, New Jersey, on July 28, 1961. Her mother, Elena Wolkonsky, is a concert-pianist and teaches at The Julliard School. Her father, the late Prince Andre Wolkonsky, a descendant of Rurik who founded Russia in 862, worked as treasurer of The Ballet Russe de Monte Carlo and later at Morgan Guaranty Trust Company in New York. One of Ms. Wolkonsky's granduncles was Mikhail Wolkonsky, director of all Imperial Theaters in Russia; the other was composer Sergei Rachmaninoff. Writer Leo Tolstoy's mother was a Wolkonsky. Prince Sergei Wolkonsky was a leader in the 1825 Decembrist uprising—the first attempt in modern Russian history to overthrow the absolute power of the czars and bring about a constitutional monarchy. The attempt was futile, but the house in which he spent thirty years of Siberian exile stands today as a cultural landmark.

When Ms. Wolkonsky was four years old, she started studying ballet with Nina Rayevskaya of the Kirov Ballet; at age five her mother began teaching her piano; at age six she was accepted to The Julliard School. At nine she began her concert career and was also accepted to study at George Ballanchine's School of American Ballet. She performed in three operas: Britten's *The Piper of Hamlin,* Ravel's *L'Enfant et les Sortilèges,* and Janacek's *Hari Janos.* When Ms. Wolkonsky was fourteen, she went to Fontainbleau, France, to study composition with Nadia Boulanger. At Julliard, she continued composing serial and neo-classical works with David Diamond. Her composition include a string quartet, a cycle of songs set to the poetry of William Blake, chamber music pieces, and orchestral works. She played piano recitals and appeared as a soloist with orchestras through 1983. Her last concert was with the Lancaster Symphony, after which she received the first Honorary Achievement Award given by the orchestra.

Later that year, Ms. Wolkonsky traveled to Russia as Special Assistant with the NBC mini-series "Peter the Great." She worked as an on-set interpreter for directors Lawrence Schiller and Marvin Chomsky. The project kept her in Russia for nine months. Upon her return to the United States, she began writing background music for Hollywood-based composer John Cacavas. Her music was used in ABC's "Lady Blue," TNT's "Margaret Bourke-White," CBS's "Police Story II: The Highway," "Portraits of Death," "Murder in Paradise," and PBS's "Confessional."

Ms. Wolkonsky is a lyricist and songwriter. She has written essays, short stories, and poetry in English and Russian. Her recordings for John Parry Music Library in Canada include original instrumental compositions, as well as classical and romantic period piano pieces. The music is used in television shows currently airing worldwide.

In private life, Ms. Wolkonsky is married to investor Nicholas C. Forstmann. They reside in New York with their daughter, Bettina.

BLOOD LINES

SECTION I: 1994

The Realm Beyond

When the invisible silence of death, with its passive words,
Whispers through the wind over the graves
Its ominous stare streaks our souls with unknown mystery.

It would not be just to give such credit to the devil
To know that Realm beyond,
If history had not sufficed us with this knowledge.

We are passing citizens in all our glory—
Every bit of charm could not exude a blossom
Or a willow from the ground.

All our faith could not restore an island to the shores of
        distant continents,
Nor jungles to the sands of deserts, nor even mountains to
        the sea.

Though they so live in harmony alone, in nature—
That most visible and living element of life
Which draws our eye and cools our breath
Or makes it hot.

Candid, we can sit and stare for hours at the blackened hills
That roll into an open ocean,
Or marvel at wild beaches growing into dense and virgin
        thick.

Yet so unnourished is our hand,
To feebly tempt or try
These rivals—we cannot.

Every day we judge our fellow man,
But never toil to meet the likes of nature proud.
This is the mother of all earthly being
And of the spheres—the face of God himself:

That purity we feel from time to time
When nothing in the world is cruel,
When motion stops, or movement plays;
When there is truth and liberty, or justice;

When things make sense, when life itself is
Both an enterprise and tiny point;
When we examine but a minute particle and feel the lines of
    life;
When music can send chills upon our skin, or paintings give
    us shivers.

This is inspiration: when we the likes of nature take
And death remains the endless pages—blank, illegible and
    void for now.

Reverie

The wind-swept crown of soft Atlantic coolness
Wet the balm of slate blue bounty.
Treasure is the movement felt in breaths
Across a smooth gold prairie;
Crisp—the sound as heavens cross
Along the very tips of dune heads dry.
Time perhaps will be forgotten,
Blown away as far,
Where suns no longer set;
When angels cease to cry.

Our walks along this nakedness of early spring
Remake the very throw and richness
Found beyond a white horizon.
Its lush, redeeming vibrance strong
Has humbly sheltered callous crows atop the thick—
An emerald green which beds the rays of evening's song;
That feather in the still: sublime as arched wings glide
The open eye through earth itself undone.

Capricious Night

Crystal stars adorned the
Onyx nights that made
The world stand still and
Time become a reverie.

The ominous and rustling
Olive branches, full of play,
Wrenching crispness, stood
Invisible and free.

The air, just hushed with coolness,
Passed atop the tarlike sea
And fingered our pallid faces,
Leaving breaths of jasmine
Towards the mossy eucalyptus trees.

They, in turn, would hiss a murmur,
Gently overshadowed by a vision:
Fire burning in the hills
Voices echoed from this
Orange glaze, whose dancing
Smoke elegantly scarved,
Then vanished into blackness.

Along the rocky cliffs
That met the sky
A greyish mist was
Left to burn our eye.

Plausible Day

When the park is bare in early December,
The thick bark which covers the trees,
Coarse as human stubbornness,
Is all that shields the woody flesh:
The harvester of spring,
The shelter of our fragile souls.

Scattered leaves, dry and brittle now
Are blown in all directions by the breeze
This mild, peculiar fall has brought.

Angry faces scorn the streets in lost emotion.
Christmas trees ignite the spirit of free enterprise
As tears roll down the soiled and tender cheekbones
Of a homeless man.

My dreams are far from being realized today
Yet God has shone his Grace on me and I am
Blessed to be a citizen of this great land.

Scars Across the Heart

Like a bursting, brilliant
Early-summer grove
Seems to fade with every season,
It never vanishes for good.

Winter only freezes our senses,
Fall just covers them with leaves,
And spring will thaw them to the
Liquid memories that quickly grow to light.

The fact that every day's a season
Can make it harder to endure.

The sorry, sad and bitter cleft
That limits our breathing
Just subsides when wallowy sleep
Takes our subconscious for a spin,

Returning once again the drill, the thinker's tool;
Leaving daybreak raw and easy like a whore.

The ones who,
Not afraid to face the
Consequence of reason,
Return to summon every year;

Defeated not by
Silent and forgotten soldiers
Faced with singular surrenders,
But by their own demise,
The greying misty mornings
And the blackness of the night.

Silent Auction

The eve of lore began to
Veil an open ocean,
Green and proud.

We sat helpless, watching
Battered fishing boats
Blend into the foamy swells.

Screeching gulls and hollering winds
Drowned the dying sailors'
Cries for liberty.

All we saw were their upturning faces
Squirm in anguish,
Open mouths and untamed gestures.

Then a block of light
Destroyed the vessels one by one.
Yellow madness filled the
Color of pure day.

Shameful silence buried
Broken parts and hinges,
Drawing them in gulps
That swallowed to the depths
Of endless treason,
Everything beneath the fee.

Verse on Love

I love you under hazy
Sunshine, when the air
Stands thick on
Summer days.

I love you in the green
Of spring, when every
Flower blooms, swaying
In the coolest breeze.

I love you in the
White of winter,
On the slopes of
Mountains rich with pride.

I love you in the
Multitude of fall, when
Auburns burst with amber punch.

Then again I love you without time,
When all millenniums have passed
And there is no more light or darkness;

Beyond our farthest
Dreams; alone, in
Terrible and trying
Supposition.

I love you in the leisure
Of a youthful spirit
And in the innocence of light,
As I do love you in the very
Shadow of unearthing death.

I love you more this
Moment, than I ever
Loved a man.
And not to make alluring promises unkept,
I love you not with words,
But with my heart.

I love you through all sorrow
And in sadness,
When weakness tempts
The strides I take.

I love you in the
Pungent, perfect
Harmony of souls
That bind together
For a lifetime.

SECTION II: 1987–88

Trains in Transit

A white foamy crown on a sapphire sea
Left a gentle smile and a memory
Before the sun had hit the trees
Already filled with summer ease.

We whisked by stacks of rolled-up hay
And sunflower fields along the way.
The sound of metal on the tracks
The scent of wood made time relax.

Faces seen in stations passed
Marked moments that we could not grasp
Yet every rock on every hill and
Every tree showed nature's will.

Far beyond the grey concrete where strangers
Pass and never meet
A red fantastic burning ball
Brings to a close night's lonely call.

A Country Road

Just after the second sunset
When a pink haze sets over the hills
And covers the prairies of gold,
The sheep into pasture are let
As the air of the day into the night spills
And all of life's stories are told.

Through this sweet night's mythical air
The stars beam a godlike stare
And challenge all else to declare
What the universe can
Through creation of man,
And the way human life takes its toll.

The Circle

The tempest growls as fierce winds blow,
Waters from their boundaries flow.
Colored red's the midnight sky,
Ravens screech while sirens cry.

Children run to find a place
Warm as Mother's kind embrace;
Couples cling in desperate love,
The elderly pray God above.

With sleep that overruns the night
Come peaceful rays of morning light;
In hue that rises from the green
Are pastel shades so rarely seen.

The gentle chirping of the birds
Like fragile rhymes of silent words
Brings up the volume of the day
Leaving millenniums to say.

But in the heat of midday sun
Human phrases become none.
There are no victors in the sands
Of deserts' vast and fiery lands.

Until the earth completes its turn
And evenings ease the day-long burn:
Just when night's bowels begin to churn,
Man thinks evil might adjourn.

Jesolo

Barely seen from thatched rooftops
Lie the marshlands hazed with blue,
Next to them abundant crops
From green fields burst each day anew.

Hammers sound a closing day,
The air like powder dries my tears;
Old villages along the way
Date back at least four hundred years.

Still standing, little churches
With inscriptions near the ground,
Ring their bells beyond the birches
To a sun no man has found.

There behind the green,
In a corner pink and gold,
All of history is seen
As its memories unfold.

Storm in Venice

In echoes of raindrops that pound on the streets
Are whispered the places where destiny meets
With all of life's wishes that set us asail,
By winds of sweet fortune that leave not a trail.

Dark purple and blue, the shadows of night
Are broken by lightning, yellow and white.
The stillness of passageways, narrow and neat,
Is cracked by the thunder that breaks like concrete.

The shutters—they rattle like a restless soul,
Hitting and scraping out of control.
Sheer curtains blow wild with cold summer rain;
From the tower, the bells ring a solemn refrain.

Here in this labyrinth, voices sound near
As feminine footsteps run faster from fear.
These glistening corridors, empty and wet,
Leave not much to say to this evening's sunset.

Faces

In the reflection of a green-grey sea,
Where children splash from lack of where to be,
Are mirrored monuments of time through art
Of which these citizens no longer are a part.

It's a pity when one so clearly sees
This regression, yes, this evident disease
From which so many suffer blindly.
Often bitter, seldom kindly,
They turn their faces in distress
As if to say the world should not progress.

A Kiss

Flower petals as the leaves will
But fall and blow away,
As the oceans and the seas
Wash the sands of yesterday.

Childhood, youth, then growing old—
Flesh with blood in the end dies,
Stars the universe can hold
Darkness, light, infinite skies:
All the things the eye can see
Cannot match a silent sound;
Love and hatred, bound and free.
Memory lost is seldom found.

Painters captured nature well,
Sculpture showed the human form,
The spheres, through music, tales can tell,
In poetry are senses born.

Yet for a feeling close to bliss,
Not words nor canvas, neither stone
Can match the music of a kiss
And all that's born from love alone.

Maybe Love

All my life I dreamt of hope.
In the beginning it was freedom;
That I would elope
And find a lead on . . .

Maybe love?

Then it changed a bit
Finding in the arts a hook:
For all comedy and wit
I realized how much it took.

Maybe love

Would once again exceed,
Searching out in me that prude,
So later on I could proceed
To build my conscience shrewd.

Maybe love

Has found its way to me
Breaking through the hopeless wild
And swimming 'cross the endless sea
To find alone this sad, old child.

Maybe love

Has been the fearless goal I
Took to conquer in my youth
And when music took its toll
I was left with but one truth:

Maybe love

Was then the golden key
To all the misery that passed.
I find these answers hard to be
But realize they're mine at last.

Just Yesterday

On a gentle, open sea I gaze;
In front of me a blank page
Of feelings lost in time
Just yesterday.

The blue aurora of life's eyes
As free as wings that glide
Through time, as if it was
Just yesterday.

Grey and pink, the granite sky
Through which I tried
To lose myself in time
Just yesterday.

Now a sigh, and not one sentiment's a lie
As felt in time
Just yesterday.

A distant fire off the coast,
A passing puff of charcoal blue
Were drenched in time
Just yesterday.

Now the world's an open book
In which we close our eyes to look
And see the sentiments we held
Just yesterday.

All the places once forsaken
Now for granted are they taken;
In our hearts they softly slept
Just yesterday.

Mountain Eagle

There's an eagle flying high
Above the city wall.
He sees the universe with its rise
And its great fall.
Gliding in the midday sun,
His worries lost, they become none.

A victim's captured every day
To satisfy his need for prey.
Sleeping high in sturdy branch,
He's got no fear of avalanche
Because his mountain is his friend
And all he's left with in the end.

After feasting on his young,
(His mating song has long been sung)
He soars alone above the land,
Diving into midnight sand.
He's buried there in his own ways;
The winds will sing his final praise.

Less Fortunate

I face the changing evening clouds,
Turn my head to silent crowds
That fill this sad and hollow space
With so much charm and so much grace.

I write to them that cannot see
Or lift their eyes and don't hear me.
For all the trouble on this earth
Cannot be healed by dollar's worth.

And all the shattered, broken hearts
Cannot be mended once apart.
We've only left to trust our souls—
That somehow they will reach their goals.

And no impatience will stand near
On the day we lose our fear;
For on that day there won't be lost
The overwhelming without cost:
Our pure existence which is life,
Our sacred vows, our endless strife.

Parting

I wallow in this sweet and tender pain;
My tears of joy I try to swallow and restrain.
Your face I see in all its splendor, all its pride
That you so well have learned to keep inside.

Each day that brought us closer to a bond
Remains today a memory so fond,
And every breath of every touch
Will still be wanted just as much

For I am left to now explain
Why I could barely feel the strain
To find another gate to cross
Another sigh and yet another loss.

September Night

Who will return
To sweep the leaves
That have already fallen
From the fingers of the trees?

Who will remember
To shut the windows and the doors
Left open by an evening storm
That flooded to the core the wooden floors?

Who will forget, enamored in the night,
The lonely walk along truth's edge?

Time will lapse
And winds will race
To find the gentle moments
When all was still in place.

Tact and gratitude
Left so ashamed
Will still endure,
But now forever maimed.

No one will try
To wipe the silent tear,
Once shed in smiling fear
From grace's cloudy eye.

There she will stand
Amidst the frost and snow
Inside a sentiment forgotten—
Her feet on icy ground.

Fate will smile as she, too, gently cries
But will not leave a trace, where once her heart did lie.

To His Memory

Father stood at window's pane,
Watching life with heavy strain,
On that grey and simple street
Where we would often meet.

I tried to hurry time
Now there's none left but mine.
One can't imagine how I felt
To watch him deal with what he dealt.

Buried deep in winter ground,
Cold and dark it must be there;
But he's far away somewhere
In a place we've not yet found.

No, it's not a flash or whim
To say how fond I was of him
And all the love I kept inside
Will to his memory confide.

SECTION III: 1995

Toward Bliss

Out across the sea,
Into the rage and fury
Part of being drives on madly
In a sweep one can't embrace.

On, through future's glory
To an undecided time and place;
Still unsure, tame contention overtakes.

Travelling the roads left passed,
On to humbler ground:
To tranquil territories yet unfound.

Edge of Light

It's there I found the knowledge of ideas
In such an isolated and uncharted moment—
Limp from all the storms of time,
Frazzled by reform and revolution,
Lashed with damnation and remorse;

Left in quiet blessing.
Onward now to face the frail yet cunning
Genius of bland semantics by offense;
The shining faces, smiling wildly
Into the brilliant glossy eyes of death

So capturing the great eternal spirit
Kept inside these darkened hills;
Those of mythical, mysterious and transient locations.
In our world ravens, swirl on blackened skies,
Circling sonic rings around a beggar's cry.

Magic Hour

The glistening grass of transparent gold
Spread revelation splendid in an hour cold.
Marking time in silent verse,
This icy bliss holds nature's very words.

How sweet the evidence
Not needing proof but this!

I saw the sunrise early on,
Now farewell magic, we move on
To night's confusion, tender, thin;
The blatant future luster wins.

A stillness other not be known
As earthly silence sung and sown.
It's music—fabric of the flying breed,
None dare question or concede.

A statement quiet amidst such antics strong
Will hold man's passions ever-long.

The Face of All-Night Sky

The distant roar of the Atlantic
Has hushed the winds of time
And left but quiet memories
To savor from a hinted past.

No longer are the evenings teary;
How far this seemingly retreated hurt has gone.
I sit and ponder on the saving
That blessed sanctity had given now.

One eye is always ever open
In case the other misses nigh,
But often there is none to relish
What all an endless night can bring.

I traced the quarantine of justice
And found that sorrow has no price:
Inside the gratitude of mourning
There lies the envy of demise.

That careful beauty, trimmed and tailored,
So often seen in modern life
Does not beguile or cool my senses
As does pure anguish and the rain.

How in the intellect of reason
Can man suffice to end his days;
The crumbling satire impending
Should serve him tribute to his fall.

When in the battlefield surrender
Tries like a sword to mark pure will,
It's few and tender that offend it
With but a strike to end it all.

In one instant of a second
Entire livelihoods can pass;
Leaving treasures in the knowing,
Throwing banners to the storm.

Through pure tyranny, entrapments
Rival conquered woes;
By the look of eyes revealing,
Read is power understood.

There can be perhaps a manner
In which otherwise this verse
Might be stated and regarded
Though by heavens not rehearsed
(Though not sung by music's lyre).

This is not the reason
Pain will strike in our hearts;
No excuses for sheer prowess
Can redeem an angry soul.

When the anima of being
Has been drained of its resource
Sleep must conjure up an answer
To replenish life's new course.

Quiet, tentative releasing
Foul and riveting response—
All the multitude of heaven
Holds a scattered, even glance.

If we open our senses
New dimensions will appear
To disregard life's mundane answers
And to dissipate its chore.

At least an ending holds no promise
As the final rhythm bears;
In that vile and horrid scandal
Profit lacks what tribute fares.

Inspiration might sustain us
But the ingenue still lives
Seeking happiness and yearning
For proximity just passed.

The rancid torment of ambition
Reigns in writing our woes;
Often not so brilliant are they,
Seldom verbalized as much.

The eyes of March affixed strong
On nature's ever-changing state
Make a prisoner of rhyme
And a chancellor of form.

Quarantined Justice

A counter-exposition of ideas I so oppose
Can be both ignorance and fury;
Irrevocable revenge which eats away
At virtue's very core.
This rage then de-humiliates the selfless being
Of some foregone predecessors to the people.
I bless them in my heart
As they in part revoke their own revealing,
While placing endless torment
On those who seek the knowledge of ideas;
Contorted, viewed so bleak, so bitter, so repressive.

A breath upon a misted morning
Cold with anger perhaps justified,
Wet with prejudice unfounded
And dampened now to ache
The bones regarded in such passive trance
Of members silent within their quiet places;
Hidden deep inside a history of man,
Not written for the few select,
But for the widows of another world;
Rejected, thrown about and severed from
The tainted common ground we tread today.

I pray and know not when
I'll see the dawn of days
Where we can look ahead
Without the excess of an
Invisible yet fervent burden
Taken so to heart
That it reduces all we know
To trifles bare and bleak.

One Day

A ruthless stranger's heart that shunned,
Then turned away its angry face,
Scarred forever lives unsaid before.
Buried underneath a rebel cause
That cries of mother's passion,
Dull remorse will never know.

I ask, yet wisdom does not speak
To tell the empty hours'
Sacred mourning. Bleak retraction,
Ever pale has not yet surfaced
In the neutered void—an unrelenting
Soul of evil born; by harshness bred
By anger sown, by silence cursed forever more.

No madness, reasoning, no dire despair
Can stop the anguish heard throughout
Our land. No heat can dry the tears
Nor is there coolness that can ease
The burn of loss tonight

When widows sleep no more
And children left without explain
Now live alone in broken song,
Forgotten harmony and endless longing
For what once was known as home.

Such agony of perished innocence
Tears wryly at the skirt of death
Brought out upon such unforgiving
Circumstance; if by the hand of friendship
Left in vain on cold, pale skulls
And broken limbs would be
Unfair, unjust, unborn.

Not Planned

Some coincidental stranger
Who drifted by and changed my
Destiny some yesteryears ago

Today had by pure chance,
Perhaps with none such symbolist intents,
Regarded me again in my own mind.

A throw of nature, blown and chipped,
(That March, most unpredictable
Revised wind of pre-spring folly)

Flared, and in an instant
Made a mark on me
So deep, so penetrating,
Odd and overly disturbing

That I rethought for but a moment
All that passed;
Revisited the early falls and
Many deaths in winters gone.

And once again returned
To prove the soul
Untamed, still wild and
Searching now anew for
Yet another temperate horizon.

In those unspeakable and fragile days—
Times I dare not recollect, yet do,
In all that readily unfolded
Still remains the truth
That austere judgment overlooked.

Now I remember
With a tender grace,
A most unwilling heart,
Such fiery rebellion had.

The tears long gone,
The visions dry,
These blessed hours
Are now truly mine.

Over Politics of Hate

In these translucent evenings,
Through the shadowy swaying of a lonely blade of grass;
Amid a sea of daisies,
Barely heard in its own whisper
Is the voice of lucid reason
Which not even thunder can erase.

With all its wisdom
Intricate yet clear,
A sigh of patience
May be all that's needed
To let this golden hour now unfold.

Pure streamlined beauty
As an unfinished thought,
Evokes the grace which
Fuschia holds in this uncharted moment.

The harshness of the outer realm,
With all its jaggedness and treason,
Could never cut into this
Wound of ecstasy sublime.

What rings a siren in a perfect heart
Will never waken mute rebellion.

This kind of liberty
Cannot be lost or tampered with
Because it knows not
Politics of hate nor
Must contend with
Self-inflicted limits on its freedom.

There are competitors in vying
(But none this day just passed)
Whose gossips render
False on all accounts.

A gentle trouble seen as massive pain
Is no complaint or lame imposter.

This voice rejects vile judgments
And brings within itself
A labor's true reward.

If I had now to wait
Another thousand years,
It would be worth the
Toil of life endured,
To even for an instant
Sense this comfort served.

It Turned to You

When silence falls upon the earth
And lunar tides will seize their flow,
I'll sing a soulful harmony
To enterprising time.

Then perhaps a praise be done—
Loose and free the call of human passions be;
I'll join my fathers in their graves
And bow a headlong fall to thee.

Until this onward spring has bloomed
With all its fragrance, colors spree;
I'll wait in lea of summer's heat,
Confide my will to heart's defeat

And mourn an only solemn call,
Aroused in winters long as midnight trains
That pass with no connection.

You will be my autumn sun,
A harvest moon, a lover young;
You will be my lonely days,
A pounding rain, a thoughtful gaze.

You will be my one retreat
From burdened life's endeavors, feats.
To you I'll sing my worldful song,
In you instilled my trust belongs.

True Wakefulness

In the dawn of days,
Where peace is my redemption,
I shall on proceed
'Til twilight's face is gone.

Through thorough pain
As in a mild and gentle pleasure,
With tears my soul rejoices:
Laughter its reward—
A sanguine child's invention.

Understanding bruises deep to all concerns;
Accept, unravel and retreat
Into the quiet line, belief alone can draw.
Then vanish in the wind that does not blow, yet is.

Try again not to see,
Or maybe doubt your judgments own;
To sleep and dream the soft, caressing
Yoke of new fulfillment known.

When they do think alike,
Side willingly against—
To break, demean, perhaps even lessen,
Strength will stand in silence,
Hold its own and never vanish.

Barely Blue

Now I approach the old familial spot
Once known in other times,
Long gone and faded to a deepened vague
Thinning in my recollection.

Tonight there is no woman who I am,
In my heart there's only poet and observer;
Shadow watcher, inspiration chaser—
Careful with the words that often spill
Like growls into the evening cool.

None left painted as the stoic column
Or a modern thought,
Up against some blurred reflections
On a prairie green;
The fingered dirt on tarnished windows—
Bright as souls that watch a vanguard dream.

Loved Another

I sat in the wilderness of night
And grieved for my reflections
On the state of history in grace,
On all a past—such glory.

None was there left the morning followed
In sadness and in yearning cupped;
Where darkness was, I walked
To breathe the summer's air
And swallow deep without retraction
Another quiet moment.

Tortured by the same reprise,
Gnawed-on by that very hurt
Which stalked me since the early days;
I knew it better than it really was
And felt it deep within the essence of Their being.

Yes, it would be what those lovers'
Dredged logic ought to feel;
Yet now, reality suppressed
Presents a different story
Which I alone should figure for my own,
Since not a soul will signal
And not a word adorn it.

Elixir of Wrath

A sorrow series—
How it sieves out from my pores
And flames this heart a burn
It knew not in forgotten times;
How hot the tearing gut
That trapped with tortured anguish,
Cramps and tears along
The walls of reason high above.

The scathing, scalding taste of liar's eyes
Inflamed as balls of burning steel
That have but neutered stale;
Stare and pierce with envy,
Wrench and reek with hatred—
Anger I've not neared so vile.

Be a lamb's or lion's heart
It cannot read to comprehend such blithe,
Sheer madness. Why—if it be known, still
Why; there is no word or motion
Which could ever justify such treason.

On a scale or from the gallows
None will reach the bald, raw evil
Burrowed in a foster claim.

My sweet burden, dry, at times
So bitter that it breaks the taste of sorrow
With a living, breathing death;
And I am healed only to convey
A weary force of goodness
In a beating pause entrenched.

Reflection's Night

Only when you sleep—
Deep inside the burrows,
The quiet tremors of your heart,
Past wild arrangements and refrains,
Into the ecstasy of pure, unsinful thought
Can be the place that homes your reason
And enchants those very senses
Still familiar, yet unknown.

When darkness sleeps,
The fiery dawn rebels;
In hours lost, the shores of man—
So driven, So exclaimed,
Drink peace and reparation
From the wet and willowy vile
That glistens in the almost light,
That parts with reason
Then embraces all a placid trance.

Within the night,
When whiteness cracks,
Enchanting fingers soft
Shall lift, and steel will bolt
This jarring furnace.

Truth shall tame then steal
A fragrant kiss from youth
And weave away repair
To times long gone.
All futures past now bow a final
Tribute to their shame.

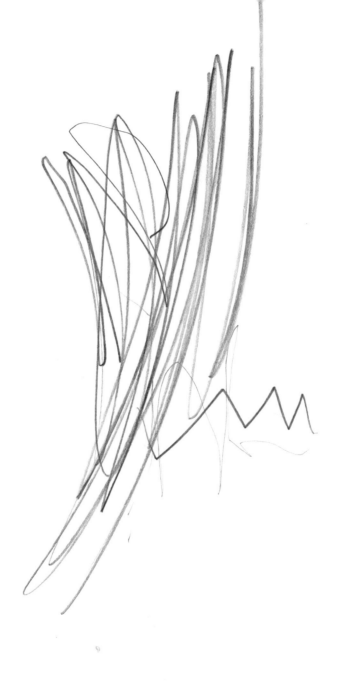